DISCARD

ANCIENT CIVILIZATIONS

ANCIENT
AZTECS

BY KAREN LATCHANA KENNEY

Essential Library

An Imprint of Abdo Publishing | www.abdopublishing.com

ANCIENT CIVILIZATIONS

ANCIENT
AZTECS

BY KAREN LATCHANA KENNEY

CONTENT CONSULTANT

Rhianna C. Rogers, PhD, RPA
Assistant Professor of Cultural Studies
SUNY—Empire State College

www.abdopublishing.com

Published by Abdo Publishing, a division of ABDO, PO Box 398166, Minneapolis, Minnesota 55439.
Copyright © 2015 by Abdo Consulting Group, Inc. International copyrights reserved in all countries.
No part of this book may be reproduced in any form without written permission from the publisher.
Essential Library™ is a trademark and logo of Abdo Publishing.

Printed in the United States of America, North Mankato, Minnesota

102014
012015

THIS BOOK CONTAINS
RECYCLED MATERIALS

Cover Photos: Fuse/Thinkstock, background; Photos.com/Thinkstock, foreground

Interior Photos: Fuse/Thinkstock, 2; Spanish School/Private Collection/Peter Newark American
Pictures/Bridgeman Images, 6–7; Photos.com/Thinkstock, 9, 47, 59, 66; North Wind Picture Archives,
13, 36, 70, 82–83; Red Line Editorial, 15 (inset), 22, 31; iStock/Thinkstock, 15 (background), 28–29,
60–61, 63, 90–91; Thinkstock, 16–17; Charles Rex Arbogast/AP Images, 20; Universal History
Archive/UIG/Bridgeman Images, 32; Dorling Kindersley/Thinkstock, 38–39, 84; Public Domain, 43;
iStockphoto, 50–51, 78; Library of Congress, 53; Werner Forman/Corbis, 55; Shutterstock Images,
68, 81, 96; De Agostini Picture Library/G. Dagli Orti/Bridgeman Images, 72–73; Biblioteca Medicea-
Laurenziana, Florence, Italy/Bridgeman Images, 75; EPA/Mario Guzman/Corbis, 85; SuperStock/Glow
Images, 94

Editor: Kari Cornell
Series Designer: Jake Nordby

Library of Congress Control Number: 2014943836

Cataloging-in-Publication Data

Kenney, Karen Latchana.
 Ancient Aztecs / Karen Latchana Kenney.
  p. cm. -- (Ancient civilizations)
ISBN 978-1-62403-535-7 (lib. bdg.)
Includes bibliographical references and index.
1. Aztecs--Juvenile literature. 2. Aztecs--Social life and customs--Juvenile literature. 3. Aztecs--
History--Juvenile literature. 4. Indians of Mexico--Juvenile literature. I. Title.
972--dc23

                                                                      2014943836

CONTENTS

CHAPTER 1   A Fateful Meeting   6

CHAPTER 2   From Mesoamerica to Aztec Empire   16

CHAPTER 3   Ruling from Tenochtitlán   28

CHAPTER 4   Aztec Society and Family   38

CHAPTER 5   Trades, Goods, and Architecture   50

CHAPTER 6   Worshiping the Gods   60

CHAPTER 7   Aztec Technology   72

CHAPTER 8   Fierce Warriors   82

CHAPTER 9   Lasting Influence   90

TIMELINE   98
ANCIENT HISTORY   100
GLOSSARY   102
ADDITIONAL RESOURCES   104
SOURCE NOTES   106
INDEX   110
ABOUT THE AUTHOR   112

CHAPTER 1

A FATEFUL MEETING

The year was 1519, and in Tenochtitlán, the greatest city of the Aztec Empire, Emperor Montezuma II received word that a fleet of ships had landed near the town of Cempoala, on the Gulf coast of what is now Mexico. Reports told of dirty and unkempt people, very unlike the Aztecs. The men had light skin, beards, and hair just to their ears. The strangers also had no

Shortly after his arrival in the Aztec Empire, the Spaniard Hernán Cortés accepts gifts from Montezuma II.

7

Hernán Cortés

Hernán Cortés, the Spanish conquistador who conquered the Aztec Empire, was born in 1485 in Spain. During the age of European exploration and colonization, Cortés left law school in Spain to seek adventure and riches in the New World. He first went to the Dominican Republic in 1504. In 1511, Cortés assisted Diego Velázquez, another Spanish conquistador of a higher rank, in conquering the island of Cuba. In 1519, against Velázquez's and the Spanish government's wishes, Cortés set sail on an expedition to Mexico. Once he arrived, Cortés discovered the Aztec civilization, which was unknown to the Europeans. Cortés became governor of the conquered lands in 1523. In 1541, he returned to Spain, where he died six years later.

regard for normal, civilized Aztec behaviors. These strangers were from Spain and their leader was Hernán Cortés.

For ten years prior to the arrival of the Spaniards, the Aztec people had witnessed a series of bad omens. Aztec legend tells of a large flash that lit up the night sky. In another omen, a temple burned from a fire that no one set. A woman's weeping cries were heard every night. She spoke of leaving the city. A dark bird was caught in some fishermen's nets. It wore a mirror on its head that reflected visions of fighting men who rode animals like deer. In yet another omen, a man with two heads and one body ran through the city. These omens stayed in the minds of the Aztecs during the Spanish arrival.

Soon a *macehual*, "common man," brought more news—Cortés wanted to meet Montezuma in the capital of the empire. On hearing the plans of these

A later artist imagined the meeting between Hernán Cortés and Aztec emperor Montezuma II in the capital city of Tenochtitlán.

newcomers, Montezuma called a meeting of his council. They decided to greet Cortés as if the visitors were royalty. The emperor sent out an embassy to travel across the land with gifts of elaborately carved discs of gold and silver. Montezuma also sent ornate ritual costumes and a gift of food, including tortillas, eggs, turkey, and maize. After greeting Cortés and his men along the Gulf coast shores, the Aztec messengers brought them back to meet Montezuma in his capital city, Tenochtitlán. The Spaniards were impressed by the gifts. They set out on August 16, 1519, to meet the emperor in his great city.

The Spaniards were prepared to fight. Their weapons were far more advanced than the Aztecs' weapons. Cortés and his men carried firearms and swords while the people they faced used darts, sling stones, and arrows.

Montezuma II

The ninth and final emperor of the Aztec Empire, Montezuma II, was born in 1466, and he took control of the empire from his uncle in 1502. Montezuma was a skilled warrior who had led many battles for the empire. As emperor, Montezuma was not only the political leader but also a religious leader. He became a powerful ruler. When Cortés captured Montezuma, the Spaniard imprisoned the ruler for months. In 1520, the Aztec people threw stones and arrows at the fallen emperor. Montezuma died shortly after, either from the stoning or from a secret strangulation.

The Spaniards wore armor and knew military drills. The Aztecs had more warriors but inferior weapons, mainly bladed clubs.

The Spaniards also had the support of warring tribes that saw the Aztecs as enemies. Cortés and his men defeated groups of native peoples along the journey, many of whom joined Cortés as his warriors. Montezuma learned of the Spaniards' approach, some 2,500 to 3,500 men strong, and decided to allow them to enter Tenochtitlán.[1] Another embassy met the men at a mountain pass close to the city. They brought more gifts, including gold necklaces, gold streamers, and long feathers.

As they approached the city, Cortés and his men were greeted with an impressive sight. They saw the gridlike order of the surrounding towns and large pyramid-shaped temples. As Cortés wrote:

When we had passed the bridge, the Señor [Montezuma] came out to receive us, attended by about two hundred nobles, all barefooted and dressed in livery, or a peculiar garb of fine cotton, richer than is usually worn; they came in two processions in close proximity to the houses on each side of the street, which is very wide and beautiful, and so straight that you can see from one end of it to the other, although it is two thirds of a league in length, having on both sides large and elegant houses and temples.[2]

The Tlaxcala People

As Cortés and his 500 men marched toward Tenochtitlán, they came upon the Tlaxcala people. These people were fierce warriors who had resisted falling under Aztec rule for years. The Aztecs attacked the Spaniards, but the Spanish weapons and military strategy destroyed the Aztec armies. After their defeat, Cortés convinced the Tlaxcalans to join him in his attempt to defeat Montezuma. Two to three thousand of these enemies of the Aztecs joined Cortés on his march. Their involvement became a major reason why the Spanish were able to conquer the Aztecs.

Montezuma gave the Spanish floral garlands, gold necklaces, and precious stones. He welcomed them to his beautiful city by giving a speech. The Aztecs provided the Spaniards a temple in which to stay. In the days that followed, the Aztecs escorted their guests around the city. A guide showed Cortés the view from atop the large pyramid. What he saw was a magnificent city below him, one much larger than any he had ever seen in Spain. After two weeks inside the city, the Spaniards began devising a plan. They would capture Montezuma and take the city, and possibly the empire, for Spain. It was the beginning of the end of the Aztecs' great civilization.

THE AZTEC EMPIRE

People have occupied the fertile highland basin in the Valley of Mexico, where Tenochtitlán was built, for more than 20,000 years. Three sides of the valley are flanked by mountain ranges. Inside, the valley is rich with water sources and vegetation. On an island

A view of Tenochtitlán as an artist imagines it looked when Cortés arrived.

13

Mesoamerican Peoples

The Aztecs were not the first great civilization in Mesoamerica. Other peoples occupied and thrived in the area for centuries, including the following:

- 1200 BCE–400 BCE: Olmecs
- 500 BCE–1000 CE: Zapotecs
- 1000 BCE–1521 CE: Maya
- 1–650 CE: Teotihuacáns
- 550–1100 CE: El Tajins
- 900–1100 CE: Toltecs
- 900–1521 CE: Mixtecs
- 1200–1521 CE: Aztecs

in Lake Texcoco was the great Aztec city, founded in 1325.

Tenochtitlán became the center of the ancient Aztec world. The Aztecs ruled over much of Mesoamerica from the 1400s to the 1500s. They developed an impressive agricultural system and became big producers, bringing wealth and allowing for a growing population. By 1519, the empire was at its height. It contained 400 to 500 city-states, covered 80,000 square miles (200,000 sq km), and had a population of between 5 and 6 million people.[3] The city of Tenochtitlán became the largest of all the Mesoamerican cities, with 140,000 people.[4] After Cortés captured Montezuma, the Aztecs fought the Spanish for nearly two years. In the end, the Spanish conquered the mighty Aztec empire, changing the course of Mesoamerican history.

The Aztec society was highly civilized, with a defined class system and organized religion, military, commerce, and courts. The Aztecs created finely decorated jewelry and intricate stone carvings. Their written language was made of pictographs. The Aztecs used mathematics and astronomy as guiding principles for city planning. The Aztec calendar was also highly evolved, coordinating with important rituals.

Today, Aztec cities and artifacts remain, leaving clues to a complex society. The Aztec language of Nahuatl remains alive and is still spoken by more than 1 million people in central Mexico.[5] Their herbal medicines, agricultural knowledge, and art continue to inspire modern cultures. Their success and later demise tell the story of the once vast and powerful empire of the ancient Aztecs.

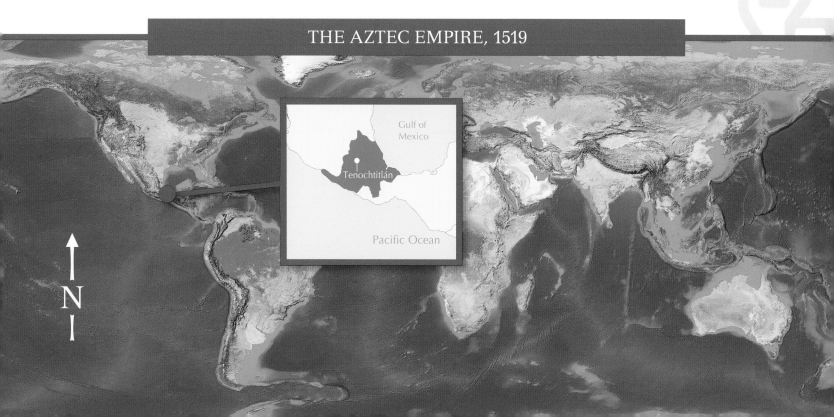

THE AZTEC EMPIRE, 1519

Gulf of Mexico

Tenochtitlán

Pacific Ocean

N

CHAPTER 2

FROM MESOAMERICA TO AZTEC EMPIRE

Long before the region between North and South America was known as Central America, it was the heart of Mesoamerica, where ancient civilizations grew and flourished. The Mesoamerican peoples built monuments and cities. They created magnificent

Toltec warrior sculptures guard the top of the Pyramid of Quetzalcoatl in Tula, Mexico.

art and music and worshiped their gods. Their societies were organized, complex, and advanced.

Humans have occupied Mesoamerica since as early as 21,000 BCE.[1] As time passed, hunters and gatherers began settling in Mesoamerica and cultivating the land, growing maize, beans, squash, chili peppers, and cotton. Agricultural villages grew into cities, forming the basis of a succession of civilizations that ruled Mesoamerica throughout the centuries.

EARLY MESOAMERICA

The Olmec civilization, which lasted from 1200 to 400 BCE, was the first highly organized society in Mesoamerica. This civilization became the basis for many new cultures in Mexico and Central America. The Olmecs developed trading routes and had a distinct artistic style, creating massive carved stone heads that still exist today. From 500 BCE to 1000 CE, the Zapotec civilization arose in the Valley of Oaxaca, where they built pyramids and palaces. The Zapotec people also developed an alphabet, a system of numbers, and their own calendar.

The Toltecs' Influence

The Aztecs greatly admired the Toltec civilization, which became an ideal and highly admired culture to the Aztecs. They modeled much of their culture after the Toltecs, including their religion and art. The Aztec term *Toltecayotl* (Toltec heart) means a person has extraordinary qualities.

Later cultures, such as the Maya and Teotihuacán, built upon the knowledge of the Olmecs. They studied astronomy, created written languages, and used mathematics. Classes divided the people, with nobility and rulers in the highest ranks. Just before the Aztecs rose to power, the Toltecs held control from 900 to 1100 CE. As this civilization declined, the Aztecs slowly rose to power.

FOUNDING TENOCHTITLÁN

In the 1200s, a wandering tribe of peoples called the Mexica searched for a new homeland. They had originally left their mythical island home of Aztlán sometime in the 1100s.[2] The name *Aztec* comes from the island's name and has become the name commonly used for the people living in the Valley of Mexico during the reign of the empire.

In the early 1300s, the Aztecs arrived at Lake Texcoco. It was a swampy area with an unoccupied island in the Valley of Mexico. The valley was an excellent place to settle. It trapped water flowing from springs, rainfall, and

A Supernatural Vision

When the Mexica arrived on the island in Lake Texcoco, one of their priests had a supernatural vision that helped convince them this was the right place to settle permanently. In his vision he saw their god Huitzilopochtli, who told the priest he would know the sacred spot where the Mexica should found their city when he saw an eagle perched on a nopal cactus. When the Mexica arrived at the island, they saw this very sight and recognized it as a sign from the priest's vision.

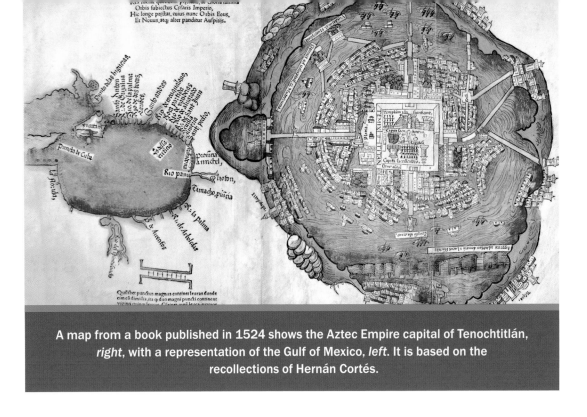

A map from a book published in 1524 shows the Aztec Empire capital of Tenochtitlán, *right*, with a representation of the Gulf of Mexico, *left*. It is based on the recollections of Hernán Cortés.

aquifers, and all this water flowed into Lake Texcoco. It was a sprawling wetland that covered 400 square miles (1,000 sq km) and had abundant wildlife and vegetation.[3]

The Aztecs claimed the island in Lake Texcoco as their final home and named the community Tenochtitlán. Although the marshy land was not ideal for farming and there were few building materials, the area was rich in birds, fish, and other aquatic life. Several communities were located on the shores of Lake Texcoco, such as Culhua and Atzcapotzalco, and Aztec women began trading fish, birds, frogs, and greens from the lake at the markets in these other communities. The Aztecs also established markets on the island, and outside communities brought goods to trade. This was the beginning of a trading network that would eventually help the Aztec civilization expand. The people also began constructing an agricultural system known as the *chinampa* system to farm food for the growing community.

From soon after the city's founding in 1325, the Aztecs' leader was Tenoch, who had been elected into office by a council of elders. Tenoch led the island community for 25 years. After his death, the new leader, Acamapichtli, brought together the people of Tenochtitlán and the people of Culhua. Acamapichtli was a noble who had both Aztec and Culhuacan ancestry.

GAINING POWER AND FORMING ALLIANCES

During Acamapichtli's rule, from 1375 to 1395, the Aztecs were subjects of a greater power in the valley. They paid tribute and were under the command of Tezozomoc from the city of Atzcapotzalco, who ruled the valley until his death in 1426. Part of the Aztecs' tribute was to fight in Atzcapotzalco's military campaigns. Eventually the Aztecs were given permission to wage their own wars to conquer towns, demand tribute, and gain agricultural lands. They continued fighting for Atzcapotzalco, proving their military

Valley of Mexico

circa 1519

Lake Zumpango

Lake Xochimilco

TEOTIHUACAN

AZCAPOTZALCO

TEXCOCO

Lake Texcoco

TLACOPAN

TLATELOLCO

TENOCHTITLÁN

CULHUA

Lake Xaltocan

Lake Chalco

XOCHIMILCO

CHALCO

might, and were rewarded with land. By 1426, the Aztecs had proven themselves equals to the warriors of Atzcapotzalco.

The new ruler of Atzcapotzalco, Tezozomoc's son Maxtla, was a murderous and volatile ruler. In 1426, he killed his brother to assume power, and then he assassinated the Aztec ruler Chimalpopoca. The Aztec council quickly elected a new leader— Itzcoatl—who was a powerful warrior. Under his leadership, from 1427 to 1440, the Aztecs sought support from neighboring cities to fight a war against Atzcapotzalco. They found allies in the leaders of Texcoco, Tlaxcala, Tlacopan, and Xaltocan. After 114 days of battle, the Aztecs and their allies defeated

This map illustrates the strategic locations of the cities belonging to the triple alliance in approximately 1519.

Atzcapotzalco and gained more power than they had ever had before, with new lands and tributes at their disposal.[4]

This war led to a 1431 alliance between three important cities in the Valley of Mexico—Tenochtitlán, Texcoco (in the east), and Tlacopan (in the west). This alliance was the beginning of the Aztec Empire, with Tenochtitlán as its capital city.

BECOMING AN EMPIRE

The fastest way for the Aztecs to increase their resources and wealth was through conquest. The Aztecs began by defeating towns surrounding Lake Texcoco. They continued onto the mainland and past the Ajusco Mountains into the Valley of Morelos. Each defeated town became a city-state of the growing empire. Each city-state had to pay a tribute to the Aztecs in the form of goods or services, which varied according to the types of resources or skills found in the area. These tributes also increased over time as the growing empire's needs increased.

In 1440, Montezuma I became the new Aztec ruler. Under his rule, the empire expanded into more distant lands. The Aztecs defeated the Huaxtecs in north-central Veracruz in the mid-1450s. They then defeated Coixtlahuaca in 1458 and moved on to defeat Cosamaloapan in 1459. By 1472, just a few years after Montezuma I died, the empire had grown to span Mesoamerica

A Great Sacrifice

When the Great Pyramid was completed in 1487, Ahuitzotl held a dedication ceremony. Atop the tall temple, Aztec priests and nobles, including Ahuitzotl, cut open and removed the hearts of 20,000 or more prisoners of war.[5] The blood of the sacrificed victims flowed down the temple steps and pooled in the square below, horrifying the Aztecs and the ambassadors invited from other nations. Human sacrifice became a powerful political tool for Ahuitzotl and future rulers of the empire.

from Oaxaca to the east along the Gulf coast to the central highlands.

Axayacatl, a 19-year-old prince, became the next Aztec ruler. His campaigns defeated towns and lands to the west of Tenochtitlán. Under his rule, the Aztecs also suffered a defeat by the Tarascans near Lake Pátzcuaro. In 1481, Tizoc came into power but did not expand the empire during his reign. Instead he focused on suppressing rebellions throughout the empire's city-states. Under Ahuitzotl, who was elected ruler in 1486, the empire took a bloodier and more ruthless turn. His mass human sacrifice at the Great Pyramid was one of the bloodiest events in the history of Tenochtitlán. His conquests further expanded the empire until 1502, when the empire's final ruler, Montezuma II, took power.

Montezuma II wanted to ensure the nobility favored him, so he created laws that exaggerated the differences between classes in Aztec society. How people dressed became even more important, so nobles could be easily distinguished from commoners. Court etiquette became more elaborate in order to show the highest levels of respect. The position of *huey tlatoani,* the Aztec emperor, gained more power, until Montezuma II was essentially a tyrant. His campaigns acquired even more territory for the empire. He also gained bitter enemies, especially in the unconquered people of Tlaxcala. By the time Cortés arrived in 1519, the empire was immense, with a population of approximately 5 to 6 million and covering an area of more than 80,000 square miles (207,200 sq km).[6]

THE SPANISH CONQUEST

Montezuma II invited Cortés, his army, and the Tlaxcalans to enter Tenochtitlán so he could watch every move his enemy made. But the Aztec ruler had miscalculated his enemy. The Spanish invaders discovered the ultimate power of the empire rested in Montezuma II. They believed capturing him was the key to the empire's fall. After Montezuma II was captured, he was taken to the palace where the Spanish and Tlaxcalans were staying. He kept up the appearance he was still ruling the city, but in early 1520 the ruler formally declared the Aztecs were the subjects of Spain.

Cortés demanded to have a Christian place of worship within the city and chose the Great Pyramid, a sacred temple for Aztec religious ceremonies. This public statement angered the Aztec people, who saw their ruler had lost his power. While Cortés was gone on a mission to Veracruz, one of his men— Pedro de Alvarado—was left in charge of the city. A large number of Aztec lords met for a ritual dance. While they were gathered, Alvarado massacred the Aztecs involved. The Spanish beheaded the drummer, stabbed others in the back, and also tore off their arms. It was a horrific slaughter.

When Cortés returned with more soldiers, the Aztecs attacked the Spanish and Tlaxcalans in their palace. When the Spanish forced Montezuma to order his soldiers to stop fighting, the Aztecs realized Montezuma was no longer a true ruler since he was now defending the enemy. When Montezuma spoke to his people a second time, the crowd jeered at him and then threw rocks and arrows at the fallen ruler. He suffered injuries and died soon after.

The fighting continued and the Aztecs took positions on the Great Pyramid, which overlooked the palace where the Spanish and Tlaxcalans were quartered. The Spanish rushed into the temple and threw the Aztec statues down the stairways and burned their shrines. The Spanish won that battle but knew they could no longer stay in the city. They escaped at night, battling the Aztecs along the causeways, but eventually did make it back to Tlaxcala. There, the Spanish and Tlaxcala rested and devised a strategy to capture Tenochtitlán.

The Spanish made allies with other Aztec city-states that were tired of submitting to the empire. Cortés convinced the leaders of Texcoco, one of the three main cities in the empire, to join him in the attack against

Tenochtitlán. The Spanish built ships to attack Tenochtitlán by water. Then, in the early summer of 1521, the Spanish and their allies attacked the city from three directions on the lake. The Aztecs fiercely resisted the Spanish and their allies, but the Spanish captured and demolished bridges and buildings, isolating the city and starving its citizens. Disease killed the newly appointed ruler and many Aztecs inside the city. The Spanish captured the city on August 13, 1521.[7] The great Aztec Empire had fallen, and the Spanish were in control. In the decades that followed, the Spanish and mixed-blood Aztecs became the nobility and rulers in the land that became known as New Spain.

Killer Microbes

While Spanish weaponry and military tactics were important in the conquest of the Aztecs, the biggest killers proved to be microbes and disease. When Cortés arrived in 1519, the Mesoamerican population was approximately 22 million. By the end of the century, that population drastically dropped to 2 million. The Spanish brought diseases the native populations had never encountered and did not have natural immunities against, such as smallpox, measles, and mumps. Other evidence suggests ticks or mosquitoes spread fatal viruses, causing several widespread epidemics.[8]

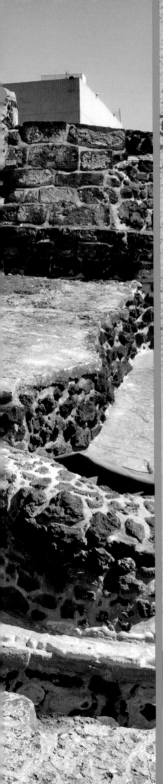

CHAPTER 3

RULING FROM TENOCHTITLÁN

The Aztec civilization had a complex system of trade, but its government sat on a shaky foundation. All power ultimately resided in one man—the huey tlatoani of Tenochtitlán. The connections between the city-states were maintained by tribute obligations, marriages between nobles, the attendance of the lords at ceremonies and other ritual duties,

The Templo Mayor in Tenochtitlán was once the physical testament to the power of the Aztec emperors.

military threats, and a legal system of standard laws and punishments. Some of these communities wanted to be free of Aztec rule, and the ultimate and singular power of the huey tlatoani led to resentment within the empire. Tenochtitlán's huey tlatoani was elevated to a godlike status—he was respected by many, but also hated and feared.

THE ORDER OF POWER

At the lowest level of Aztec government were the calpulli. This was a group of families that collectively owned land. Many calpulli were part of a city, called an *altepetl*. Each calpulli had a leader who collected taxes and made sure the group's children received an education.[1] These calpulli leaders were members of the altepetl's council. From that council, four members formed a higher council. Its leader was the altepetl's *tlatoani*, the highest leader of the city. The tlatoani served in his position for life.

The empire itself was an alliance between the three city-states—Tenochtitlán, Texcoco, and Tlacopan—with Tenochtitlán as the dominant arm of the alliance. Each of the three city-states in the alliance was ruled by a tlatoani. In these large city-states, the tlatoani was the head of external affairs of the government. He served as head of the military, oversaw the temples and markets, resolved judicial issues, and ultimately owned all of the land in the city. The tlatoani's council included the *cihuacoatl*, the

Aztec City Government

```
                    ┌─────────────────────┐
                    │      TLATOANI       │
                    │  AND HIGH COUNCIL   │
                    └─────────────────────┘
                              │
                    ┌─────────────────────┐
                    │      ALTEPETL       │
                    │       COUNCIL       │
                    └─────────────────────┘
              ┌───────────┴───────────┐
    ┌──────────────┐            ┌──────────────┐
    │   CALPULLI   │            │   CALPULLI   │
    └──────────────┘            └──────────────┘
```

TLATOANI AND HIGH COUNCIL

ALTEPETL COUNCIL

CALPULLI

CALPULLI

FAMILY OR INDIVIDUAL

FAMILY OR INDIVIDUAL

FAMILY OR INDIVIDUAL

FAMILY OR INDIVIDUAL

FAMILY OR INDIVIDUAL

FAMILY OR INDIVIDUAL

head of internal affairs of the government. He was the supreme judge for the courts, and he appointed lower judges and handled financial matters for the city. Below the tlatoanis and cihuacoatls were appointed rulers who governed different districts. Aztec nobles held most positions of power in the government. All were ultimately responsible to the head of the empire—the tlatoani of Tenochtitlán, known as the huey tlatoani.

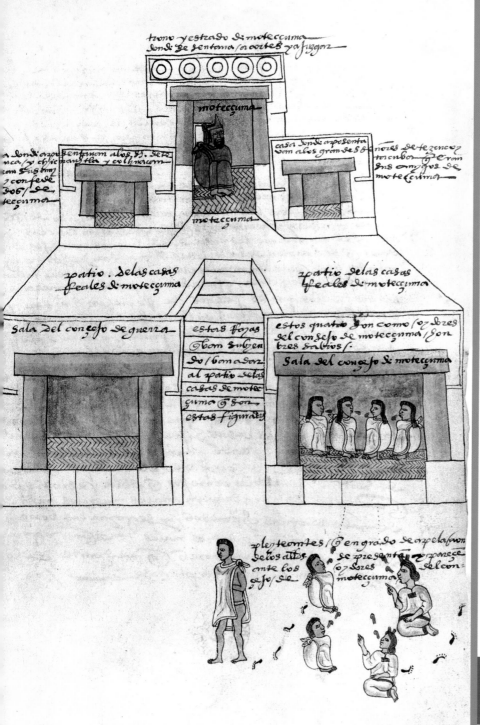

Conquered cities remained fairly independent within the empire, and many local rulers were allowed to keep their positions. Once a part of the empire, though, the cities were required to pay tribute to Tenochtitlán. At its height, the empire contained 38 provinces.[2]

PAYING TRIBUTE

Each community in the empire paid tribute to the government. This is how the government secured and grew its wealth. The tributes were made with specific types of goods

Montezuma II sat at the top of Aztec government, with the four judges of the high council in the middle and the commoners at the bottom.

or services, usually based on the skills or resources common to an area. Some valuable tribute items included jaguar skins, exotic feathers, and cacao beans. Every year Tenochtitlán received an enormous amount of goods from the empire's communities, which included 7,000 short tons (6,300 metric tons) of maize, 4,000 short tons (3,600 metric tons) of beans, and 2 million cotton cloaks.[3]

Tribute List

According to the *Codex Mendoza*, this is what the 23 towns in the province of Petlacalco were required to give to the empire:

Every six months:

- 400 multicolored loincloths
- 400 women's tunics and skirts
- 2,400 large white mantas (a blanket shawl or cloak)
- 400 white mantas with multicolored borders
- 400 diagonally divided mantas

Once per year:

- 1 blue quaxolotl warrior costume and shield

- 1 blue cuextecatl warrior costume and shield
- 1 white and red tzitzimitl warrior costume and shield
- 1 yellow ocelotl warrior costume and shield
- 1 green xopilli warrior costume and shield
- 20 red warrior costumes and shields
- 20 red cuextecatl warrior costumes and shields
- 20 blue papalotl warrior costumes and shields
- 1 bin of beans (a bin equaled 6,300 to 7,875 bushels [220 to 280 cu m])
- 1 bin each of chia, maize, and amaranth[4]

Tax collectors had an important role, making sure each community paid its tribute in full at the required times of year. Failure to pay a tribute could result in death or destruction of property. The tax officials carried tribute goods back to Tenochtitlán, where they were used for the empire's needs such as religious ceremonies, or sold at markets or given away as gifts. The amount of the tributes increased over time, leading to resentment among some of the city-states.

LEGAL SYSTEM

The Aztecs had a system of laws and punishments created to strengthen the government's central power. This system was introduced by Netzahualcoyotl, the tlatoani of Texcoco from 1431 to his death in 1472. The laws defined behaviors and responsibilities of Aztec citizens and also clearly defined the punishments for breaking those laws. Often the punishments were severe and absolute.

Laws were based on royal decrees and long-standing Aztec customs. Judges applied these laws in the Aztec court system. Aztec laws were written using pictographs on sacred *amatl*

Lost Laws

Many Aztec laws and aspects of the legal system are unknown now because these laws were just being formally written down at the time of the Spanish conquest. The Spanish destroyed many Aztec legal records and documents, using some as fuel for fires. Others were neglected and allowed to rot, and more were destroyed because they went against the new society the Spanish wanted to establish.

paper made from bark that showed the type of crime committed, such as stealing, and its prescribed punishment, which in the case of stealing was strangulation. There were 80 laws in the Texcocoan legal code, and similar laws were used in Tenochtitlán.[5]

CURRENCY AND TRADE

Aztec currency was in the form of goods. The Aztecs used a bartering system in which some objects had generally accepted values throughout the empire. These objects included cacao beans, cotton cloaks, and transparent quills made from feathers that were filled with gold dust.

Cacao Beans

Cacao beans are the fruit of the cacao tree, a tropical evergreen that is native to rain forests in the Amazon and Orinoco river basins. The beans grow in long pods filled with 20 to 60 beans each. These beans were ground into powder and used to make a chocolate drink prized by the Aztecs. Nobles drank the chocolate with added chili water, flowers, vanilla, bee honey, or other flavorings. One hundred cacao beans could buy a fine cape. Sixty-five cacao beans could buy a manta. Cacao beans were even counterfeited. The counterfeiters formed earth into the shape of a bean and then covered and sealed it with a cacao husk. Cortés brought cacao back to Spain, where it became popular among the nobility. The Spanish sweetened the cacao and added vanilla and cinnamon, serving the drink hot. The Spanish later introduced the chocolate drink to Italy, France, and other European countries.

Aztec merchants worked their way up and down the canals of Tenochtitlán, selling and trading goods.

Goods from across the empire were sold in the greatest marketplaces of Tenochtitlán and its suburb Tlatelolco. Every day, more than 60,000 people visited the market in Tlatelolco, the commercial center of the empire.[6] Market inspectors roamed the marketplace to regulate prices and to ensure all trading was fair. All kinds of luxury goods could be purchased at the market, including jade, turquoise, copper tools, tobacco pipes, vanilla, and chocolate, just to name a few. Slaves were also commonly sold in markets.

Long-distance trading was also an important aspect of the Aztecs' economy. Traders, called *pochteca*, traveled to areas far outside the empire's lands on trading missions. Some were regular traders, others were commissioned by rulers for their personal business, others dealt only with slaves, and some acted as spies for the rulers. The Aztecs set up trading centers in towns around Mesoamerica. Some routes stretched up to present-day Arizona and New Mexico. Other routes led to the Gulf coast and Maya towns. Some trade went as far as South America. These traders exported Aztec goods such as copper bells, combs, obsidian ornaments, and rabbit-fur skins. They returned with exotic feathers, animal skins, gold, and valuable stones. This flow of goods fed the Aztec culture and government, providing for the needs of its many citizens.

Trader-spies

Marketplaces were also centers of gossip. Some traders, called the *naualoztomeca*, acted as spies along their trading routes. They changed their dress, hair, and speech to better fit in while visiting enemy territories. The information they brought back to the huey tlatoani was vital. The government often sent out these trader-spies before an Aztec attack.

CHAPTER 4

AZTEC SOCIETY AND FAMILY

In the complex social system of the ancient Aztec world, class, familial duties, and roles were strictly defined. Laws governed what members of different classes and different genders could wear and do. Failure to follow this social system could result in serious punishment or even death.

A typical Aztec lakeside dwelling included mud walls and a thatched roof.

THE NOBILITY

The highest class in ancient Aztec society was the *pipiltin*, or nobles. The pipiltin included military and government leaders, high priests, and lords. They owned land and received tribute from the lower classes. The status of nobility was passed on through family lineage.

Nobles could also display their wealth through their appearance. They wore fine jewelry and elegant clothing. Only nobles could wear cotton garments, shoes, and certain colors. For example, only Montezuma II could wear a turquoise cloak. The nobles owned art and had large houses and

Aztec Beauty and Hygiene

Cleanliness and looks were very important to the Aztecs. Many bathed at least once a day, using certain fruits and roots as a kind of soap. Women wore perfume and applied yellow makeup to their face and limbs. The makeup was made from either yellow clay or *axin*, a substance made from insects.

Hairstyles were also a sign of class, age, or trade. Most male commoners wore their hair short with short bangs. Some priests wore their hair long and tied back in a white ribbon. Men of different trades had distinct hairstyles. Women had many different hairstyles as well. Mothers, for example, wore their long hair tied back in a ponytail. The loose ends were pinned up at the top, making a tuft of hair at the crown of the head. Some also dyed their hair using the herb *xiuhquilitl* or mud, giving it a purple shine.

many servants. They were also allowed to eat certain foods commoners were not allowed to eat.

COMMONERS

Below the nobility were the commoners, called the *macehualtin*. This class included the rest of the free people living in Aztec society, such as the merchants, peasant farmers, and artisans. The macehualtin worked for the nobility, attending to their palaces, farming their lands, and fighting in their wars. They paid taxes in the form of tribute to the tlatoani and belonged to a calpulli, which owned communal land that was passed on from one generation to the next.

Commoners could only wear clothing made from fibers rougher than cotton, such as maguey, yucca, or palm. Male commoners had to tie their capes at the shoulder, while nobles tied them in the middle of the chest. And the capes worn by commoners had to stop at the knees, while nobles could wear this garment to their ankles.

Social rank also existed within the commoner class. Merchants and highly skilled artisans were above the peasant farmers. Although commoners could become very wealthy, they could never join the noble class. Sometimes nobility would marry commoners. The couple's children inherited the noble status from the noble parent.

A CLOSER LOOK

THE *CODEX MENDOZA*

One way historians now know and understand Aztec culture is through studying Aztec codices. Codices were made before and after the Spanish arrived, but none survived the conquest. The Spanish burned them, believing they contained anti-Christian content. The codices made after the conquest recorded important information about Aztec practices and culture.

The Codex Mendoza is one important codex created 20 years after the Spanish conquest. It was commissioned by the first Spanish Viceroy of the conquered empire, between the years 1535 and 1550. It contains three sections. The first section details an account of the rulers of Tenochtitlán. The second section lists the tributes given to the capital from more than 400 towns. The third section recorded Aztec life.

One page of the codex, *right*, shows how spies were used to gather information about an enemy city. The spies are at the top of the page, shown visiting all parts of the city. The middle shows the Aztec official with a shield and arrows behind him. He is speaking with the people he will later defeat in battle. The lower section shows four great Aztec captains—

Tlacatécatl, Tlacochcálcatl, Huiznáhuatl, and Ticocyhuácatl. The information is presented through Aztec pictographs with annotations in Spanish.

Ollama

A ball game, called *ollama*, was played in large ball courts in Aztec cities. The game was filled with Aztec symbolism. The courts were shaped like a capital *I* and faced either north-south or east-west. Stone walls defined the sides of the court, and each side had a stone ring. The game used a small, hard rubber ball. The court symbolized the heavens; the ball was a symbol of the sun, moon, or stars; and the rings represented the sunrise or sunset. Players wore padding and tried to hit the ball through the rings using their elbows, hips, or knees. It was a violent game, and players were likely to be seriously injured or killed. The game also had ritual significance, and players were sometimes sacrificed.

THE LOWER CLASSES

At the bottom in social rank were the landless serfs, or *mayeque*, and slaves, or *tlacotin*. The landless serfs were free people who did not own land and did not belong to a calpulli. The mayeque were bound to the noble's land where they worked as tenant farmers, fishermen, or artisans. They paid the noble for use of his land with a portion of their harvest, catch, or goods created.

Slaves also served their owners and did not own land, but they were not free. They became slaves for several reasons. For some, slavery was a punishment for a crime, such as theft. Others became slaves due to unpaid debts, and still others were captured during war. During times of extreme hardship, such as a drought or famine, parents sold their children into slavery. Slavery was a temporary position though, and freedom could be bought back at a later time. Slave owners were required to feed and clothe their slaves, and slaves had to work for their masters for no pay. Slaves could marry, and their children were born free.

FAMILY LIFE

Aztecs married in their late teens or early twenties. Matchmakers and parents arranged the marriages between young men and women. Nobles often married to create alliances or for profit. The bride was ceremonially bathed and covered with red feathers; her face was painted in glittering crushed pyrite, a gold-colored mineral. Four days of feasting followed the marriage ceremony, and elders counseled the bride and groom.

Once married, the husband and wife had clearly defined roles. The man was the head of the family, but women were regarded as equals. While men worked in their trades, women held mostly domestic roles. They could not speak publicly or have the careers men had, but they did have a level of independence. Female commoners wove cloth to sell at the market and to be given for their family's tribute. A wife ground maize for five to six hours a day to feed her family. She cleaned the home and took care of the family's animals, among many other duties. Noblewomen had a much different life, with servants to do the many things a commoner wife would do to run the household. Nobles had time for many leisure activities.

Motherhood was a woman's most valued role in Aztec society. Parents were dedicated to rearing their children properly. Children were raised to respect their elders and their religion, have good manners, and become productive citizens. By the age of three or four, children were given specific chores within the household. Between eight and ten years old, children learned different crafts, such as pottery, metalwork, and basketry. Aztec parents could punish misbehaving children harshly. In the *Codex Mendoza*, different punishments were listed. Pinching arms or ears was a common punishment. More severe punishments included making children inhale

Newborn Ceremony

Childbirth was a very special event in Aztec life. If a mother died during childbirth, she was honored as a warrior for fighting a good battle during the delivery. Babies were treated as weary travelers who had just arrived into the world. The midwife gave formal speeches while cleaning the baby. A boy's umbilical cord was later taken by a warrior to be buried on a battlefield, and a girl's cord was buried near the hearth in a family's home. Family and visitors came to see the child, sometimes visiting for up to 20 days after the birth. To provide the child with a good start in life, a soothsayer would assign an astronomically favorable day for the child's naming ritual. The naming ritual, conducted by the midwife, ended the newborn ceremonies. A feast was held at the end of the ceremony, and the child's parents gave gifts to the visiting family.

the fumes of roasting chilies or tying them up and leaving them outside in the mud or cold.

EDUCATION AND SCHOOLS

Education was a very important part of Aztec life, and both boys and girls attended school. Aztec children were promised to schools as infants but did not begin school until later. Children typically began school between the ages of six and nine, but sometimes formal education began as late as 15 years old.[1] There were two kinds of schools,

Aztec boys and girls learned a number of different household chores, including weaving cloth, grinding maize, and loading and steering a canoe.

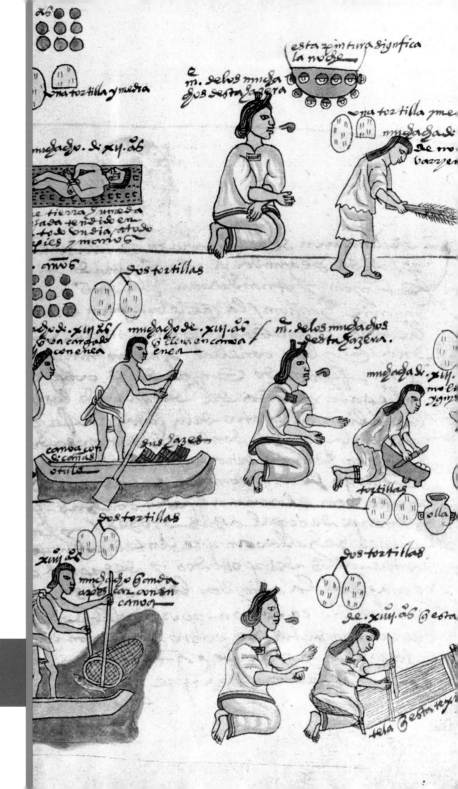

Poetry, Language, and Dance

Poetry, language, and dance constituted an important part of Aztec education. Metaphors were essential in formal public speaking. Ritual ceremonies, songs, and dances were filled with metaphors, some so complex that instruction was necessary in order to understand what was being shown or explained. All members of Aztec society took part in different ceremonies. Understanding how to dance, sing ritual songs, and interpret ceremonies was a vital part of daily life.

and in each boys and girls were separated to reinforce gender and social differences.

One kind of school was the *telpochcalli*, for commoner boys and girls. Each calpulli had its own telpochcalli, so there might be many of these schools in one city. Children learned history, basic moral and religious values, ritual dancing and singing, and the language arts, including public speaking skills. The boys' instruction included military training, while the girls learned how to participate in religious ceremonies and traditions in which adult women served. Memorization was an important skill to have. Rhythmic language and drumbeats helped students learn poetic language and songs.

The second type of school was for the children of nobility—the *calmecac*. Sometimes the brightest commoner students were specially chosen to attend these schools as well. In each city there was only one calmecac for boys and another for girls. Students were trained for military, religious, or political leadership roles. It was a very strict atmosphere, similar to a military academy. Students learned how the Aztec calendar worked and about the many religious festivals and ceremonies. They also learned reading, astronomy, history, math, architecture, agriculture, basic law, and warfare.

LANGUAGE AND SCRIBES

The written form of Nahuatl, the language spoken by the Aztecs, consisted of hieroglyphics and other symbols. Scribes worked for palaces, law courts, temples, schools, and trading centers. They wrote on folding *amatl* paper manuscripts and used numbers, figures, date signs, and hieroglyphics. They wrote historical records, tribute lists, calendars, laws, and descriptions of professions and daily life. This writing was also used on monuments and sculptures. By the time the Spanish arrived or soon after, much of Aztec culture and history was written with this system in codices, such as the *Codex Mendoza*. These records preserved important information about how Aztec society and its government worked in the time before the Spanish conquest.

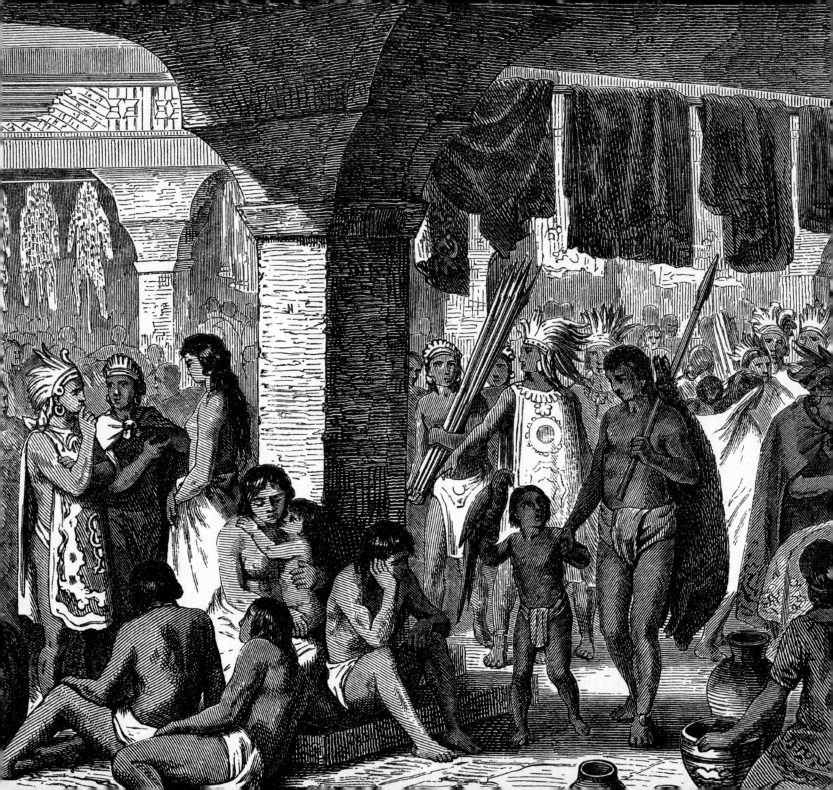

CHAPTER 5

TRADES, GOODS, AND ARCHITECTURE

After school, Aztecs moved on to their professions and began contributing to Aztec society. Nobility served in leadership positions, such as in the military and as high priests. Commoners took positions in service trades or became farmers or tradesmen.

At the marketplace, Aztec men and women sold everything from vegetables they had grown to the cloth they had woven.

FARMERS, TRADESMEN, AND ARTISANS

Farming was central to Aztec society. Farmers used a sophisticated farming system to grow the food needed to feed the empire's large population. Their crops included maize, beans, amaranth, and tomatoes. Farmers worked the land and tended to the crops. A higher-level farmer, called a horticulturalist by the Spanish, understood the importance of rotating crops each year and knew how to transplant and seed different plants.

Tradesmen worked with precious stones, using obsidian knives to cut and create intricate mosaics and masks. Other stone workers sculpted slabs of rock into large figures. Carpenters crafted the wooden furniture for the nobles' patios and homes. They also made canoes, flat-bottomed boats, and drums. Feather workers dyed feathers and created beautiful mosaics on shields, headdresses, cloaks, and flags. Basket makers wove all sizes of baskets from reeds, leaves of different plants, and cane. People used baskets to store grains or carry food. Fine baskets held valuable items in the home, such as jewelry.

Other tradesmen wove reeds into mats used on floors in Aztec homes. Metalworkers formed gold into beautiful and delicate jewelry, adding jade, crystal, or turquoise.[1] Cloth workers made a variety of cloth from cotton

Aztec women prepare offerings of maize and cups of chocolate for the gods. Maize was central to the Aztec way of life.

and fibers from the maguey cactus. Pottery workers made everyday items, such as clay griddles for baking tortillas, as well as finer pieces meant for use in temples. Vendors at the marketplace sold the many goods and foods produced locally as well as goods that traders brought from far away.

A CLOSER LOOK

TURQUOISE MOSAIC MASK OF XIUHTECUHTLI

This Aztec mask is believed to represent the sun god Xiuhtecuhtli. The mask, which measures 6.5 inches (16.8 cm) tall and 6 inches (15.2 cm) wide with a depth of 5.3 inches (13.5 cm), has a wooden base that is covered with a mosaic of turquoise stones, mother-of-pearl shell, and white conch shell. The individual pieces were glued to the mask using pine resin. The eyes are carved from mother-of-pearl shell and gilded with a very thin sheet of gold. The mask's teeth are carved from white conch shell.

The mask also features raised turquoise bumps that look a bit like warts. Experts believe the warts may mean the mask represents the god Nanahuatzh, who had boils, or large bumps, all over his face. According to Aztec legend, when the universe was taking shape, Nanahuatzh jumped into a huge fire and became the sun.

Holes located at the top of the mask suggest it was made to be worn. The mask, which has been on display at different locations in the United Kingdom

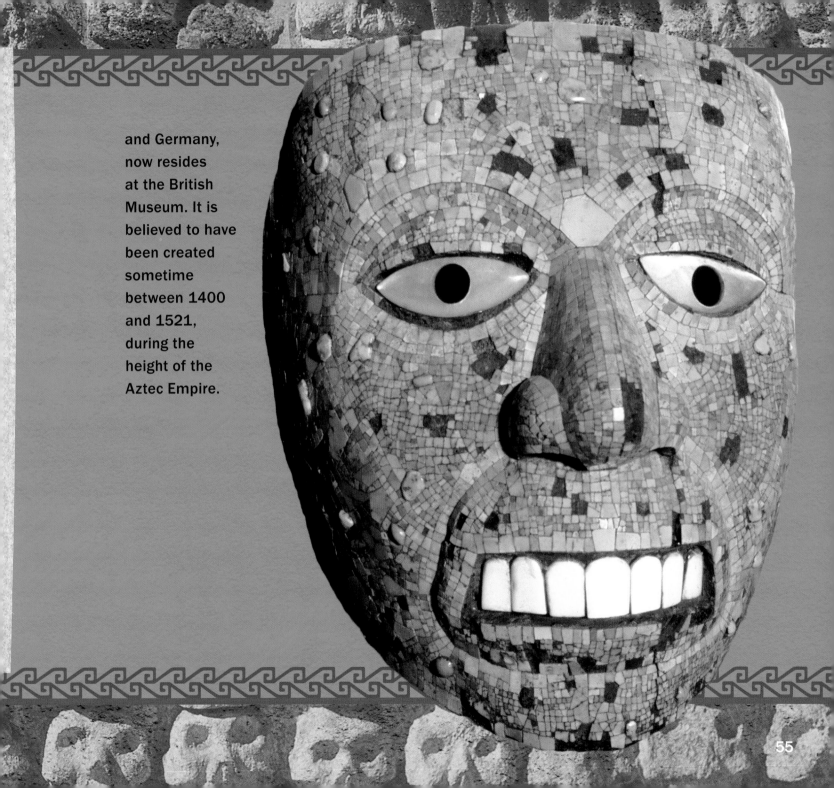

and Germany, now resides at the British Museum. It is believed to have been created sometime between 1400 and 1521, during the height of the Aztec Empire.

Alcohol and the Aztecs

The Aztecs practiced moderation in many aspects of daily life, so public drunkenness was not acceptable in their society. *Octli* alcohol was only permitted on certain occasions, and people were not allowed to drink more than four cups at a feast. Drunkenness was punished severely, sometimes with a sentence of death. Only elder commoners were allowed to drink as much octli as they wanted, and they could drink outside of ceremonial occasions as well.

THE AZTEC DIET

One could find a variety of foods at the market—from squash and beans to tropical fruits to deer and rabbit. The main staple in the Aztec diet was maize, used to make tortillas and tamales. The Aztecs developed many different tamale recipes with various kinds of fillings, showing the sophistication of their cuisine. Popcorn was also an important part of the diet. The *Florentine Codex* lists many Aztec recipes.

The Aztecs raised only a few kinds of animals for food, including turkey, duck, and dogs, along with bees for honey, so vegetables and fruits made up the bulk of the commoners' diet. Meat and fish were reserved for the nobility. Some other sources of protein included salamanders, tadpoles, and insects. Amaranth, a high-protein grain, combined with beans gave Aztecs much of the protein they needed.

Vegetables included different kinds of squash, tomatoes, sweet potatoes, jicama, and nopal cactus. Greens were also an important part of the diet.

The Aztecs had many kinds of fruit to choose from as well, including guavas, avocados, papayas, and custard apples, just to name a few. Different spices flavored their foods—from epazote, used with beans, to different chilies and vanilla.

Chocolate was a prized drink among the nobles. Alcohol was not used by the nobles but was acceptable for older commoners to drink. From the fermented sap of the maguey cactus, the Aztecs made a lightly alcoholic drink called *octli*.

ARCHITECTURE AND MONUMENTAL ART

Aztec cities were filled with a variety of buildings—from simple common homes to multiroomed royal palaces and impressive public buildings. The Aztecs reused architectural styles from neighboring peoples and predecessors to show their power, especially from the great empire of Teotihuacán. Laws prohibited commoners from building homes more than one story tall. Their homes contained two or three rooms built around a central courtyard. Many

Montezuma's Meals

While Aztec commoners ate two simple meals a day, Montezuma II enjoyed meals of variety and extravagance. He sat behind a gilt screen so that others could not see him eat. Young maidens served him several hundred dishes at each meal. Dwarfs, jugglers, and acrobats also entertained the ruler while he ate. Montezuma ate at a table covered with a white tablecloth using white napkins. These were luxuries no commoner could afford.

were built from wattle and daub, a construction method using mud and sticks. Nobles had the privilege of building homes that were two stories tall with many rooms, made from cut stone.

Most Aztecs had little furniture inside their homes. They slept on mats on the floor or on dirt platforms and had a chest in which to store clothing. Nobles may have had curtains around their sleeping areas and murals painted on the walls. Montezuma had more furniture. He sat in a wooden chair and used a dining table.

RELIGIOUS STRUCTURES

Temples were very important religious structures within Aztec cities. Made from stone, some temples sat on platforms atop large pyramids with steep stairs leading up to the temples. The Great Temple in Tenochtitlán is one of the finest examples of Aztec architecture.

Many fine and impressive stone sculptures were created for Aztec temples. The images they depict are both terrifying and powerful. The massive statue of Coatlicue reaches a height of more than eight feet (2.5 m) and depicts the Aztec earth goddess with two fanged serpents where a head should be. Her necklace is made of human hearts and hands with a skull at its center, and her skirt is made of writhing snakes. Another famous sculpture is the large stone disk of Coyolxauhqui. It shows a dismembered

Aztec warriors defend Templo Mayor, the Great Temple, in Tenochtitlán against Spanish attacks.

goddess with monstrous masks on her knees, elbows, and sandals. Death was a common theme in large Aztec sculptures, which were painted in bright colors.

CHAPTER 6

WORSHIPING THE GODS

Almost all aspects of the Aztecs' culture revolved around pleasing their gods and following rituals to assure good health, harvest, and prosperity. The Aztecs developed a world of myths, symbols, and signs that followed a strict schedule of feasts, sacrifices,

Masks of Quetzalcoatl, the plumed serpent, decorate the side of the Temple of Quetzalcoatl in Teotihuacan.

pilgrimages, and ceremonies. It became their rhythm of life, marking the changing seasons and the passage of time.

GODS, HEAVENS, AND THE UNDERWORLDS

The Aztecs practiced polytheism, meaning they worshiped many gods. Some gods belonged to certain communities. After conquering new cities, the Aztecs adopted these different gods into their main religion and ceremonial cycle. This was one way to link the peoples of the Aztec empire. All gods had ties to nature, from the waters and rain to fire and the sun. The Aztecs believed the gods controlled every part of their lives.

Although the Aztecs had many gods, some gods held a higher status within their mythology. Tezcatlipoca, or Smoking Mirror, was a very powerful god linked with the powers of destiny and fate, war, and sorcery. Quetzalcoatl, or Plumed Serpent, was the patron of priests and the god of life and who created humans. Another very important god was Huitzilopochtli, or Turquoise Prince, the sun and war god who was often shown as a hummingbird. The Aztecs believed this god needed to be nourished each day with human blood. Tlaloc was the rain god, who could make droughts and famine happen or provide the people with rain for bountiful harvests.

The Aztecs also believed in a layered system of heavens and underworlds. Thirteen layers made up the heavens, with the god Ometeotl ruling over the universe. The sun, moon, stars, comets, and winds occupied lower heavens. The earth sat in between the heavens and underworlds. Below the earth were nine underworlds. Souls had to pass through the layers to reach their final resting place.

AZTEC PRIESTS

Since religion was so important to the Aztecs' culture, Aztec priests held positions of power with great responsibility.

A massive statue of Tlaloc, the Aztec god of rain, is on display at the National Museum of Anthropology in Mexico City.

63

Priests came from all social classes, but the highest priests had noble blood. They directed all religious ceremonies and festivals, influenced the arts and literature, and governed the schools. They also vowed to be celibate and kept their hair long and matted with blood. Their skin was marked with cuts made in offerings to the gods.

Priests had many different roles within the priesthood. The highest served just under the ruler. Under them, another level of priests was in

The Five Suns

The Aztecs believed Earth experienced five ages of destruction and rebirth. They called each age a "sun." The myth of the five ages was recorded on the Stone of the Five Suns and in the *Codex Chimalpopoca*.

The first age was called four jaguar. This was a time when giants walked the earth. They did not farm or grow maize but ate fruits and roots. The age ended when a jaguar killed and ate all of the giants. The second age was called four wind. The imperfect humans of the time turned into monkeys when a fierce wind swept over the earth. The third age, called

four rain, ended with a rain of fire, and its people died or were changed into birds. Rain dominated the fourth age, called four water, and its people were turned into fish. The fifth age is the current age, called four movements. The sun, moon, and humans came into existence at the beginning of this age. Aztec prophecy predicts this fifth age will end with earthquakes.

To create humans, Quetzalcoatl descended to the underworlds. He found the bones of different imperfect humans and crushed them. Then the god sprinkled his blood on the crushed bones. This act created the perfect human beings of the Aztec culture.

charge of specific temples and their related festivals and sacrifices. There were also priest-warriors, who carried religious icons into battle. Some lower priests served as codex painters and scribes. They studied astronomy and interpreted Aztec almanacs. Other priests predicted the future or interpreted visions caused by certain hallucinogenic plants. Some priests served as wise men and teachers who read and owned books and were leaders. Although the Aztec priesthood was mostly male dominated, there were some female priests who served in the earth goddess cults and performed duties related to maize goddesses.

Venus and Astronomy

To make their intricate and accurate calendars, Aztec priests studied the sun, moon, planets, and stars. Venus was the most important planet to the Aztecs. They believed it was a symbol of Quetzalcoatl. When it was shining at night, Aztecs feared its rays, believing they projected illness or death upon those who watched it.

BLOOD AND SACRIFICE

Blood and human sacrifice was an integral part of Aztec religion, and almost every important ritual involved a human sacrifice. The Aztecs believed the gods needed to be nourished and repaid for creating the earth and the sun with offerings of blood and the life energy of humans. They thought this gave the gods the energy to continue the natural cycles on which the Aztecs depended, such as the seasonal cycles and the sunrise each morning.

A page from an Aztec codex illustrates a human sacrifice at an Aztec temple.

An alternative to sacrifice was bloodletting. Aztecs would cut their ears or legs to offer their blood to the gods.

Scholars believe between several hundred and several thousand men were sacrificed in Tenochtitlán each year.[1] The need for these sacrifices drove the military into battle, which expanded the empire as well. Captured enemy warriors became the ideal sacrifices for upcoming rituals. Other sacrificial victims were chosen and trained to impersonate certain gods as part of a ritual. They lived as the gods for a time and were later sacrificed. Sometimes babies, children, and women were also sacrificed for specific rituals, although mostly warriors were killed. After the sacrifice, the skulls of the victims were publicly displayed on skull racks near the temples.

AZTEC CALENDAR AND RITUALS

The Aztec calendar organized time and dictated the rituals of Aztec life. Daily life, festivals, and large-scale events all followed the calendar. An important ceremony marked each month, and citizens had duties to prepare for each one.

Sacrifice for Tetzcatlipoca

A young, handsome captured warrior was chosen each year to be the sacrifice to Tezcatlipoca during the month of *Toxcatl*, the dry season. The man was trained to play the flute, sing, arrange flowers, and speak and act as the deity. He lived in luxury for a year and was treated as if he were a god. During the last 20 days of his life, the young man was given four wives. The wives symbolized the goddesses of love, corn, salt, and water. Together they represented the five parts of the universe.

On the day of the sacrifice, the man climbed to the top of the temple dedicated to this ceremony. The priests cut out his heart and raised it up in an offering to the sun. Then they cut off his head, removed its contents, and hung the skull on a skull rack for public display.

The Aztecs had two calendar systems. One was the *tonalpohualli*, which marked a 260-day cycle. This calendar, which was separated into 20 groups with named and numbered days, was used as a sacred and divine almanac. One part of the cycle had names, such as rabbit or jaguar, while a second part of this cycle was numbered from one to thirteen. Both calendars were marked on rotating disks, which aligned to show the corresponding name and number for each day. Priests used pictographs to record the counts of these days and their corresponding ceremonies and rituals.

The tonalpohualli calendar was recorded on amatl screen-fold books, called *tonalamatl*.

The second calendar was called the *xiuhpohualli*. It had 365 days per year and was divided into 18 months of 20 days each. This calendar recorded annual festivals and events. There was also a five-day period called *nemontemi* at the end of each year Aztecs believed to be a very dangerous and unlucky time. These five days did not belong to a month. The Aztecs stayed in their homes and did not cook over fires in order to stay hidden from the attention of bad spirits. Each xiuhpohualli year took its name from the tonalpohualli day on which it began and a number from one to thirteen. Because of the way the calendars intersect, there were four possible names: rabbit, reed, flint knife, or house. The years had a 52-year cycle before the year-number names were repeated. The end of an old and beginning of a new cycle was a very important event in Aztec society.

Each month was dedicated to a ritual. These rituals fell into three main categories. One type focused on mountains and water and ensured the rains

Aztec Calendar Stone

Buried by the Spanish after the fall of the Aztec Empire, an Aztec calendar stone was uncovered in 1790 in Mexico City. The images on the stone depict the Aztec calendar. At the middle of the stone is the face of the Aztec sun god. Four panels around the god's face show the four previous ages of the Aztec world, part of the culture's creation myth. Around the four panels is a circle of symbols that represent the 20 days of the Aztec month.

fell. Another type was for fertility and abundant harvests. These ceremonies were done for the sun, earth, and maize. The third type celebrated and honored certain gods. Other rituals did not follow the calendar. They were performed for certain life events, such as death, marriage, and birth. These rituals were celebrated with feasts, dancing, music, and pageantry.

TEMPLES AND SACRED PLACES

The sites where many Aztec rituals took place were of great importance. In addition to providing a main place of worship, temples were the hearts of Aztec cities. They sat on pyramids that rose high above the cities, like mountains, inspiring awe and

The Aztecs gathered in temples, such as the Temple of the Sun, to worship their gods.

reverence. Long, steep staircases lined the sides, and sacrifices were often performed at their summits.

Many sacred places existed outside of cities as well. Mountains and hills were sacred places because they provided water. Caves were also considered to be sacred sites. The Aztecs believed caves were the entrances to the underworlds. Temples and shrines were often built for worship and ceremonies at these sacred Aztec sites.

Mountains of Life

Two mountains were sacred places for rainmaking rituals in the ancient Aztec world—Mount Tlaloc and the Hill of Tetzcotzingo. Both mountains rise near the city of Texcoco. The temple atop Mount Tlaloc's summit sits at 13,000 feet (4,000 m).[2] A long corridor leads to a rectangular temple, both with walls that once stood 10 feet (3 m) tall. Spanish texts explain the temple was a place of pilgrimage. Aztecs visited the temple in April or May of each year to perform a ceremony that was meant to summon the rains. Inside the temple was a thatched wooden structure with different stone idols.

The ritual Hill of Tetzcotzingo was designed to align with the cosmos. A walkway below the summit leads to four ritual baths cut into the rock at northern, southern, eastern, and western points. Aqueducts supplied the baths with water, which was used to purify visitors. Shrines were placed around the hill. At the summit is the Tlaloc mask—a carved boulder showing the image of the rain god Tlaloc.

CHAPTER 7

AZTEC TECHNOLOGY

I t took centuries to build the Aztec Empire, and as it grew, so did the Aztec people's mastery of different types of technology. Aztecs used math to measure distances, lengths, and land area. Their technological advances focused on practical use, such as farming and building. Aztecs used obsidian and copper tools to build, carve, and sculpt using stone and wood.

The Aztecs invented a number of ways to live on and around water. Island gardens called chinampas allowed them to grow most of the food they needed.

73

Canoes and Boats

A dugout canoe was very useful for navigating the canals and lake surrounding Tenochtitlán. These canoes were made from hollowed-out logs burned by fire. Aztec carpenters also made a flat-bottomed boat similar to a raft, consisting of planks of wood tied together with tight fibers.

From this knowledge, the Aztecs built an impressive array of tools, structures, and systems to help their society thrive.

TRANSPORTATION

While the wheel was used only for toys and there were no beasts of burden, the Aztecs developed several ways to transport goods long distances. The most common form of transporting goods was in a woven cane container strapped to a person's back on a carrying frame. Porters, called *tlamemes*, specialized in this type of transport. Each tlameme could carry a little more than 50 pounds (23 kg) for approximately 13 miles (21 km).[1]

Travelers navigated between cities along a system of roads. The most developed roads were located near cities. A main highway linked the major cities in the empire. Local peoples or authorities maintained the sections of road located near their towns.

In Tenochtitlán, five great causeways connected the city to the mainland. People could walk along the causeways over the lake to travel outside of the city. These 12-foot- (3.7 m) wide causeways consisted of wooden stakes

In this illustration from the *Florentine Codex*, a midwife applies an herbal remedy to an Aztec woman who has just given birth.

driven into the lake bed and filled in with sand, dirt, and rocks.[2] To allow the current to flow throughout the lake, parts of the causeways were cut away, creating canals. Over those gaps sat wooden bridges.

HERBAL MEDICINE

With tropical forests as their backyard, the Aztecs had a cornucopia of plants with which to experiment for their medicinal and healing properties.

As a result, the Aztecs became expert herbalists, with remedies for many ailments—from a simple headache to a head wound.

Aztec physicians were educated and very experienced. They made hundreds of prescriptions for different types of wounds, diseases, and other health issues. These physicians knew of the many herbs, stones, trees, and roots with healing properties that could be used to treat specific ailments.

Some conditions needed more than herbal prescriptions, though, and physicians also knew how to perform different procedures. They could extract teeth and prevent tooth infections. They could also treat

The *Badianus Manuscript*

By the time the Spanish arrived, the Aztecs had been practicing medicine for centuries. These expert herbalists had extensive knowledge about the medicinal uses of plants. In 1552, two Aztec scholars recorded a list of herbs used by their people in the *Badianus Manuscript*, which was written in Nahuatl and later translated into Latin.

The Aztecs had specific medicinal mixtures to treat many kinds of ailments. To stop a nosebleed,

Aztecs mixed juice from a nettle plant that was ground in salt with urine and milk and poured this mixture into the nostrils. For a lightning strike, an injured person drank a liquid made from the leaves of different trees and rubbed a plaster made from different herbs on his or her body.

head wounds by cleansing the injury, applying different salves, and then wrapping the wound with a bandage. The Spanish noted how effective Aztec physicians and medicine were and sent doctors from Spain to learn about their techniques. Many of these herbal treatments are still used in Mexico.

AGRICULTURE AND WATER

Swampy land is not ideal for farming, but the Aztecs succeeded in making the area around the island city of Tenochtitlán agriculturally productive. They built raised farming beds called chinampas on the shallow lake bed. To construct a chinampa, first a rectangular area was chosen and its four corners marked with wooden stakes extending into the lake bed. The size of the chinampas ranged from approximately 10 to 16 feet (3 to 5 m) wide and 20 to 98 feet (6 to 30 m) long.[3] The rectangular area was then filled with layers of mud and vegetation. The finished chinampa extended approximately 3 feet (1 m) above the water. Willow trees were planted at each corner to help stabilize the chinampa. Sometimes farmers also built their homes on these plots.

Fertilizer for the Chinampas

The Aztecs were model organic farmers who did not let anything go to waste—even human excrement. They filled canoes with excrement from the dwellers of Tenochtitlán and sent the canoes to the chinampa fields. This human waste was then used as a rich fertilizer for the soil.

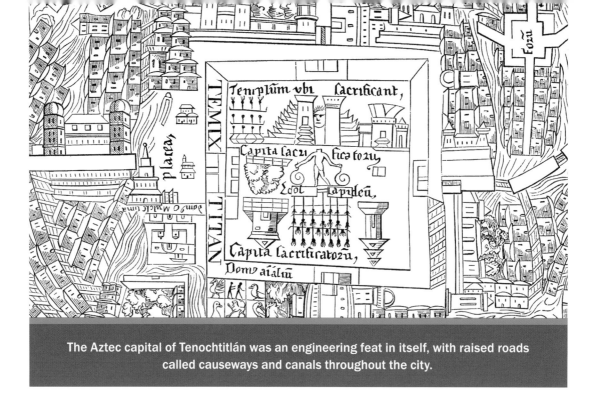

The Aztec capital of Tenochtitlán was an engineering feat in itself, with raised roads called causeways and canals throughout the city.

Even though they lived on a lake, the residents of Tenochtitlán needed clean drinking water and water to irrigate farms. Some of the water in the lake was saline, and therefore undrinkable. Aztec engineers devised an ingenious type of aqueduct to bring freshwater into the city. The Chapultepec aqueduct originated at the Chapultepec springs and ended in the city's center. It was built on a raised platform, running atop a causeway near the city. At its base were wood pilings, topped with a sand, lime, and rock foundation. This base supported two masonry water channels. While one channel was in use, the other could be cleaned and maintained. This ensured the water flow never stopped. The Chapultepec aqueduct was the most advanced aqueduct the Aztecs built, but they built many other aqueducts during their rule.

CITY PLANNING

Building on the urban styles of the earlier cities of Teotihuacán and Tula, Aztec city planners carefully thought out the design for the Aztec capital. Its design was so awe-inspiring that Spanish explorers called it the "Venice of the New World."[4]

The city was divided into four quarters, each representing north, south, east, and west. The ceremonial center was considered the fifth direction, a religious symbol of what the Aztecs believed held the sky and earth together. Each quarter was further divided into four quadrants. These smaller neighborhoods belonged to different calpulli, and each had its own central plaza. Canals crisscrossed the city as well, following a geometrical pattern using right angles. These many technological advancements made the Aztec capital an impressive sight. It became the admired and inspired heart of the empire.

Construction Methods

From houses to palaces, the Aztecs used a similar template for their construction. A standard design consisted of rectangular rooms built around a central courtyard. Outer walls were made from wood or stone, and roofs were straw thatch or flat stone. Inside, the walls were covered with wooden planks, latticework with adobe plaster, adobe bricks, or stone. The marshy conditions in Tenochtitlán also caused buildings to sink, so builders raised many homes on stone platforms.

A CLOSER LOOK

TEMPLO MAYOR

At the center of Tenochtitlán was the immense pyramid-shaped Templo Mayor, reaching a height of 150 feet (46 m).[5] Atop its summit were twin temples, one dedicated to the god Tlaloc and the other to the god Huitzilopochtli. This temple was built and rebuilt over several centuries, increasing in size as the city grew.

The first simple temple was built in 1325 and then rebuilt to a height of 49 feet (15 m) in 1390.[6] In approximately 1431, the temple was rebuilt again. The new pyramid enclosed the old pyramid. In 1454, under Montezuma I, the pyramid was improved again and many decorative elements were added. New stairs and a greenstone sculpture adorned the temple and its grounds. It was further rebuilt in 1482, 1486, and 1502. Today the temple is sinking into the marshy soil that makes up the foundation of Mexico City.

CHAPTER 8

FIERCE WARRIORS

Warfare brought more than just newly conquered lands into the empire—it also brought additional tribute and captives, many of whom were doomed for sacrifice. The military was essential to meeting the many needs of Aztec society, and being a warrior was considered a sacred duty. In fact, new rulers proved their strength with a war. Before being

On June 30, 1520, Aztec warriors attacked the Spaniards in Tenochtitlán during La Noche Triste, which means "night of sorrow."

confirmed, a new ruler had to lead a coronation war to bring new lands, tribute, and sacrificial captives for the empire. Their triumphs were carved in stone to mark their coronation.

All newborn boys, whether they were commoners or nobles, were treated as warriors during the newborn ritual. Boys' military training began during school. They learned different maneuvers, military drills, and how to handle weapons. And they began gaining real experience by carrying loads for warriors during military campaigns. Eventually the trainees worked their way up to becoming true warriors.

A young Aztec apprentice warrior, in traditional battle gear, holds a spear-thrower, shield, and stone-point darts.

TYPES OF WARRIORS

The Aztecs' military structure conformed to a strict hierarchy of power. Success on the battlefield meant warriors moved higher up in rank and status. Although a warrior who was a commoner could not become a noble, he could reach a quasi-noble status with certain rights and privileges and wealth. At the highest level, the tlatoani and a supreme council decided when to go to war. The council was composed of four noblemen, and in Tenochtitlán these council members were either brothers or close relatives of the tlatoani.

Eagle warrior statues, found near Templo Mayor, once guarded the doors to a chamber where the warriors met.

Noblemen or commoners who had achieved military success held lower positions of office.

The Aztec military was divided into ranks based on achievements on the battlefield, such as the number of captives a warrior caught during battle. The highest military ranks were the jaguar and eagle societies, and the warriors who belonged to these societies were the best warriors in the Aztec military. To be accepted into the jaguar and eagle societies, a warrior had to have captured four enemy warriors and performed 20 deeds showing

Warrior Costumes

A warrior's costume had to be earned. Aztecs knew a warrior's accomplishments simply by looking at his attire. The length and color of one's lip plug showed the number of distinguished captives taken on the battlefield. Feather headdresses, cloaks, and leather sandals showed a warrior's rank and could only be worn by those awarded permission by the tlatoani.

In the *Codex Mendoza*, different costumes are described for warriors who had captured a certain number of captives. A warrior who had captured two enemies could wear an orange cloak with a red border. A warrior who had captured three enemies wore a cloak with a distinctive design and a special border. He also carried a blue-bordered shield and a war club. The jaguar warrior's costume consisted of a spotted suit with a helmet shaped like a jaguar's head. Eagle warriors wore eagle-shaped helmets and suits that were covered with feathers.

great bravery.[1] Society members achieved a high level of honor and respect in Aztec society.

AZTEC WEAPONS

Warriors used several kinds of deadly weapons during battles. A throwing spear used an atlatl—a special grooved tool that gave warriors better accuracy and power. The spears and darts used in an atlatl were made from wood with sharp points tipped with obsidian, metal, or fishbone. Bows and arrows and slings were also important weapons used by the Aztecs. Leather-covered round shields protected warriors from enemy blows.

One of the more deadly weapons used was the *macuahuitl*.

This Aztec warrior of the jaguar society wears the traditional battle costume.

Obsidian Blades

The Aztecs didn't use much metal in their weaponry. Some ax blades were made from copper, but none were iron or bronze as it was not readily available. Instead, the Aztecs used obsidian, a natural black glass. This glass is stronger than steel and easily breaks into sharp blades. Mesoamerica had abundant sources of obsidian, which the Aztecs used in many types of weapons and tools.

This was a wooden war club edged with obsidian blades. Most were approximately 3.5 feet (1.1 m) long, but some were so big a warrior had to use the club with both hands.[2]

GOING TO WAR

There was no standing army in the Aztec Empire. Instead, when the tlatoani and council decided to wage war, warriors from the calpullis were called up for service. Calpullis in Tenochtitlán had to contribute 400 warriors each. Combined, a basic unit of the army had 8,000 warriors.[3] Many units were called up for a battle, along with porters to carry supplies. The tlatoani also gave orders to towns to provide the army with battle supplies. Towns sent maize cakes, beans, chilies, pumpkin seeds, and other food items to the capital.

The army set out by foot to approach the enemy town. Small winding trails crossed the rural countryside. Warriors traveled in single file, with a basic unit stretching for approximately 15 to 20 miles (24 to 32 km) along the trails.[4] As they approached the battlefield, the army was an impressive sight. Warriors dressed in full costume spread out across the battlefields. The Aztec battle strategy was basic man-to-man combat, charging upon the enemy and fighting duels between experienced warriors. Thousands of men raised their voices in war cries, whistles, and howls. Aztec warriors set fire to the roof of the main pyramid temple in the conquered town—a true symbol of defeat. The warriors then pillaged the town, taking what they could and securing their captives. To secure peace, town leaders had to agree to pay a tribute to the empire.

Flower War

Another form of battle was a military ritual called a Flower War, a staged war performed to capture warriors for sacrificial purposes and to train warriors in the art of battle. Leaders from both sides agreed to these ritual wars before they occurred. These rituals were regularly held between certain cities in the empire. The wars showed the strength of the Aztec army and intimidated enemy warriors. Sometimes these flower wars were all that was needed for the Aztecs to capture a city.

CHAPTER 9

LASTING INFLUENCE

W hat was once the heart of the Aztec Empire is now the heart of Mexico—Mexico City. The capital of Mexico was built from the ruins of Tenochtitlán, Tlatelolco, and the Spanish colonial settlement. It is now the largest city in the Western Hemisphere. The country's Aztec past resurfaces

This series of skulls, carved into a wall at Templo Mayor, was unearthed when the site was discovered in the early 1970s in Mexico City.

Mexican Flag and Currency

Mexico has adopted Aztec myths and symbols in its national flag and currency. The flag features the country's national emblem, which shows an eagle eating a serpent while sitting on a nopal cactus. This symbol is based on the legend of the founding of Tenochtitlán. Each of Mexico's coins also shows a part of the designs found on the Aztec calendar stone. An illustration of the Aztec ruler of Texcoco, Netzahualcóyotl, is also on the Mexican 100 peso bill.

constantly, through archaeological discoveries, art, and its living language and people.

SPANISH RULE

After the fall of the Aztec Empire, the Spanish began colonizing what is now central Mexico. Christianity was a driving force used by the Spanish to rule the Aztecs. The Spanish razed Aztec temples and religious centers, building cathedrals and missions in their place. Templo Mayor was dismantled, and the Metropolitan Cathedral of the Assumption of Mary of Mexico City was built in its place. The Aztec system of rituals was destroyed, breaking apart the social structure of Aztec society. Spanish became the main language spoken throughout New Spain. Cities adopted Spain's political systems, and the tribute system was used to support Spain. The Spanish ruled Mexico for the next 300 years, until Mexico gained its independence in 1810.

AZTEC RUINS

While the Spanish destroyed many Aztec pyramids, artworks, and sculptures, some structures were well preserved. The most well-known ruin is Templo Mayor, the ceremonial center of Tenochtitlán. Much of it was buried when the Spanish built their city atop the Aztec city. After its discovery in 1978, the site was heavily excavated over the next five years. Workers found seven layers showing the great temple's construction phases. More than 100 sacrificial deposits were found, containing more than 6,000 Aztec objects.[1]

New Aztec objects and ceremonial sites are constantly being unearthed by archaeologists as the city builds roads or begins other construction projects. Today, visitors can see many Aztec artifacts and learn about the culture in Mexico's museums, including the Templo Mayor Museum and Mexico's National Museum of Anthropology. Many museums around the world also contain collections of Aztec art and sculpture, and touring exhibitions teach viewers about the Aztecs.

Amazing Discovery

A crew of electrical workers was doing some routine maintenance in a Mexico City street in 1978 when they made a monumental discovery. They found a giant round stone showing the goddess-warrior Coyolxauhqui. The crew knew they were in the archaeological zone and contacted the Mexican authorities. It turned out to be one of the most important Aztec archaeological finds to date.

MODERN ARTISTS

Aztec mythology and symbolism have influenced many Mexican artists.

World-famous muralist Diego Rivera referenced the Aztecs in many murals and sculptures. His murals at Mexico City's National Palace depict the history of Mexico. One mural, called *The Great City of Tenochtitlán*, shows the Aztec city's market, temple, and people.

Another beautiful example of Rivera's Aztec-influenced artwork is seen in his *Fountain of Tlaloc*, the Aztec rain god. This giant mosaic-tiled sculpture was built between 1950 and 1952 at a pumping station for the Mexican municipal water system in Chapultepec Park. It shows Tlaloc lying on his back in a shallow pool with his arms and legs splayed around him. Rivera also painted colorful and intricate murals along the floor of the tank.

Miguel Covarrubias was a Mexican illustrator, researcher, and writer. Much of his illustration, painting, and writing focuses on the peoples of Mesoamerica. Nobel Prize–winning poet Octavio Paz also wrote about the Aztecs. His epic poem *Piedra del Sol* is about the Aztec sun stone and the Aztecs' worship of Venus.

A LIVING CULTURE

The Nahua peoples are the descendants of the Aztecs. They are mostly rural farmers living in Mexico, and they grow many of the foods once cultivated by the Aztecs, such as maize, maguey cactus, and squash. More than 1 million people still speak Nahuatl, the ancient language of the Aztecs.[2] Mexican Spanish includes 3,000 words that come from this language, including

many plant and instrument names.[3] Different Aztec foods have endured as well—enchiladas, tamales, and chocolate are just a few. In markets, healers sell healing herbs and plants used in Aztec times. Chinampas can still be seen in the town of Xochimilco, where many plants and flowers are grown.

The Aztecs were the largest civilization in Mesoamerica. They built a vast empire and dominated the Valley of Mexico for centuries, leaving behind many artifacts and structures, as well as a living culture that continues to influence modern ones. New artifacts from this ancient civilization continue to be discovered, revealing new secrets and teaching us the ways of the ancient Aztecs.

Guacamole

One lasting food from the time of the Aztecs is guacamole. They called it *ahuaca-mulli*, Nahuatl for "avocado sauce." The Aztecs made this sauce very much as guacamole is made today, mashing avocados with tomatoes, onions, and cilantro.

Modern Aztec descendants perform at Xocalo Square in Mexico City on February 23, 2010.

TIMELINE

21,000 BCE
Humans first occupy Mesoamerica.

1325 CE
The Mexica people found Tenochtitlán.

1325
Tenoch rules over Tenochtitlán for 25 years.

1431
Tenochtitlán, Texcoco, and Tlacopan form a triple alliance.

1440
Montezuma I takes control of the Aztec Empire.

1458
The Aztecs defeat the city-state of Coixtlahuaca.

1459
The Aztecs defeat the city-state of Cosamaloapan.

1466
The Aztecs' final ruler, Montezuma II, is born.

1472
The Aztec Empire spans Mesoamerica from Oaxaca to the Gulf coast and the central highlands.

1486
Ahuitzotl becomes tlatoani and makes human sacrifice even more important to the empire, using it as a political tool.

1487

Approximately 20,000 people are sacrificed at the Great Temple's dedication ceremonies in Tenochtitlán.

1502

Montezuma II becomes the tlatoani of the Aztec Empire.

1519

The Aztec Empire covers an area of 80,000 square miles (210,000 sq km) and has a population of 5 to 6 million people.

1519

Hernán Cortés meets Montezuma II and sees the great Aztec Empire.

1520

The Aztec Empire becomes a subject of Spain; Montezuma II dies after his people hit him with stones and arrows.

1521

The Aztecs and Spanish battle for 93 days around Tenochtitlán, with the Spanish capturing the city on August 13.

1552

The *Badianus Manuscript* is written, detailing herbs and remedies used by Aztec healers.

1950–1952

Artist Diego Rivera creates the *Fountain of Tlaloc*, which shows the Aztec god of rain.

1978

Electrical workers find the Coyolxauhqui stone, beginning excavations that lead to the discovery of ancient Aztec ruins of the city of Tenochtitlán.

ANCIENT HISTORY

KEY DATES

- **1325 CE: Tenochtitlán founded**

- **1431: Tenochtitlán, Texcoco, and Tlacopan become allies**

- **1502: Montezuma II becomes the tlatoani**

- **1519: Hernán Cortés meets Montezuma II**

- **1520: Montezuma II dies**

- **1521: The Spanish conquer Tenochtitlán**

KEY TOOLS AND TECHNOLOGIES

- Aztec farmers developed organic farming techniques, chinampas, and the cultivation of maize, beans, and other plants.

- Artisans exhibited fine metalwork techniques and precise stone carving in statues and monuments.

- Aztec engineers used advanced building techniques for large pyramid temples and palaces, as well as aqueducts, canals, and other types of water manipulation techniques and roads, causeways, and bridges.

- Aztec healers developed medicine and the use of different healing herbs and plants.

LANGUAGE

Nahuatl

CALENDARS

- The *tonalpohualli* calendar had a cycle of 260 days. It was divided into 20 groups of 13 days each, with named and numbered days.

- The *xiuhpohualli* calendar had a cycle of 365 days. It was divided into 18 months of 20 days each, plus a five-day period at the end of each year (*nemontemi*). Each year was named.

- It took 52 years for the two calendars to complete a cycle together.

IMPACT OF THE AZTEC CIVILIZATION

- Artifacts are seen around the world through museum exhibitions, and codices preserve vital information about the culture.

- Many Mexican artists have been influenced by the Aztecs' religion and art.

- The Aztec language is still spoken by more than 1 million people.

QUOTE

"When we had passed the bridge, the Señor [Montezuma] came out to receive us, attended by about two hundred nobles, all barefooted and dressed in livery, or a peculiar garb of fine cotton, richer than is usually worn; they came in two processions in close proximity to the houses on each side of the street, which is very wide and beautiful, and so straight that you can see from one end of it to the other, although it is two thirds of a league in length, having on both sides large and elegant houses and temples."

—*Hernán Cortés*

GLOSSARY

aqueduct
A structure that conducts large amounts of water from one area to another.

artisan
A worker who specializes in a certain trade or craft.

campaign
A series of military battles.

causeway
A raised road that allows for travel across marshy land or water.

codex
A manuscript book.

commoner
A person who is not of noble blood.

decree
An order enforced by law.

elder
An older person who has authority because of age and experience.

hieroglyphics
Writing done using a series of symbols and pictures.

lineage
Descent from an ancestor.

microbe
A small organism or germ.

scribe
A writer or person who copies documents.

tribute
A payment from a city-state to a more powerful nation.

ADDITIONAL RESOURCES

SELECTED BIBLIOGRAPHY

Aguilar-Moreno, Manuel. *Handbook to Life in the Aztec World*. New York: Oxford UP, 2007. Print.

Berdan, Frances F. *Aztec Archaeology and Ethnohistory*. New York: Cambridge UP, 2014. Print.

Berdan, Frances F., and Patricia Reiff Anawalt, eds. *The Essential Codex Mendoza*. Berkeley: U of California P, 1997. Print.

Phillips, Charles. *The Art & Architecture of the Aztec and Maya*. London: Annes, 2007. Print.

Townsend, Richard F. *The Aztecs*. 3rd ed. London: Thames & Hudson, 2009. Print.

FURTHER READINGS

Buckley, A. M. *Mexico*. Minneapolis, MN: Abdo, 2012. Print.

Heinrichs, Ann. *The Aztecs*. New York: Marshall Cavendish, 2012. Print.

Olhoff, Jim. *The Conquistadors*. Minneapolis, MN: Abdo, 2012. Print.

WEBSITES

To learn more about Ancient Civilizations, visit **booklinks.abdopublishing.com**. These links are routinely monitored and updated to provide the most current information available.

PLACES TO VISIT

SMITHSONIAN NATIONAL MUSEUM OF AMERICAN HISTORY

Fourteenth Street and Constitution Avenue, NW

Washington, DC, 20001

202-633-1000

http://americanhistory.si.edu

Visit this museum to see Aztec artifacts and modern art reflecting Aztec style.

TEMPLO MAYOR MUSEUM

8 Seminario Street

Cuauhtemoc, Mexico City, Mexico, DF, 06060

(55) 4040 5600

http://www.inah.gob.mx

This museum contains the many Aztec artifacts found in the archaeological zone of Templo Mayor.

SOURCE NOTES

Chapter 1. A Fateful Meeting

1. Richard F. Townsend. *The Aztecs, Third ed.* London: Thames & Hudson, 2009. Print. 228.

2. Hernán Cortés. "Cortés on Meeting Moctezuma." *Cartas y relaciones de Hernán Cortés al emperador Carlos V.* Ed. Pascual de Gayangos. Paris: A. Chaix, 1866. *American Historical Association*. Web. 4 Sept. 2014.

3. "Aztec." *Encyclopaedia Britannica.* Encyclopaedia Britannica, 2014. Web. 4 Sept. 2014.

4. Ibid.

5. "Nahuatl: An Uto-Aztecan Language of Mexico." *Endangered Language Alliance.* Endangered Language Alliance, 2012. Web. 4 Sept. 2014.

Chapter 2. From Mesoamerica to Aztec Empire

1. "Mesoamerican Civilization." *Encyclopaedia Britannica.* Encyclopaedia Britannica, 2014. Web. 21 May 2014.

2. Richard F. Townsend. *The Aztecs, Third ed.* London: Thames & Hudson, 2009. Print. 54.

3. Ibid. 8.

4. Ibid. 73–74.

5. "Ahuitzotl." *Encyclopaedia Britannica.* Encyclopaedia Britannica, 2014. Web. 26 May 2014.

6. "Aztec." *Encyclopaedia Britannica.* Encyclopaedia Britannica, 2014. Web. 4 Sept. 2014.

7. Richard F. Townsend. *The Aztecs, Third ed.* London: Thames & Hudson, 2009. Print. 237.

8. Bruce Stutz. "Megadeath in Mexico." *Discover.* Kalmbach, 21 Feb. 2006. Web. 5 Sept. 2014.

Chapter 3. Ruling from Tenochtitlán

1. Rebecca M. Seaman, ed. *Conflict in the Early Americas*. Santa Barbara, CA: ABC-CLIO, 2013. Print. 153.

2. Ibid. 154.

3. Michael D. Coe and Rex Koontz. *Mexico: From the Olmecs to the Aztecs, 6th ed*. New York: Thames & Hudson, 2008. Print. 199.

4. Frances F. Berdan and Patricia Reiff Anawalt, eds. *The Essential Codex Mendoza*. Berkeley, CA: U of California P, 1997. Print. 34–36.

5. Richard F. Townsend. *The Aztecs, Third ed*. London: Thames & Hudson, 2009. Print. 90.

6. Michael D. Coe and Rex Koontz. *Mexico: From the Olmecs to the Aztecs, 6th ed*. New York: Thames & Hudson, 2008. Print. 194.

Chapter 4. Aztec Society and Family

1. Richard F. Townsend. *The Aztecs, Third ed*. London: Thames & Hudson, 2009. Print. 184, 193.

Chapter 5. Trades, Goods, and Architecture

1. Michael D. Coe and Rex Koontz. *Mexico: From the Olmecs to the Aztecs, 6th ed*. New York: Thames & Hudson, 2008. Print. 204.

Chapter 6. Worshiping the Gods

1. Richard F. Townsend. *The Aztecs, Third ed*. London: Thames & Hudson, 2009. Print. 137.

2. Constance Holden. "How Aztecs Did Math." *AAAS: Science*. American Association for the Advancement of Science, 2014. Web. 5 Sept. 2014.

SOURCE NOTES CONTINUED

Chapter 7. Aztec Technology

1. Manuel Aguilar-Moreno. *Handbook to Life in the Aztec World*. New York: Oxford UP, 2007. Print. 341–342.

2. Charles Phillips. *The Art & Architecture of the Aztec and Maya*. London: Annes, 2007. Print. 58.

3. Frances F. Berdan. *Aztec Archaeology and Ethnohistory*. New York: Cambridge UP, 2014. Print. 80.

4. Manuel Aguilar-Moreno. *Handbook to Life in the Aztec World*. New York: Oxford UP, 2007. Print. 227.

5. Charles Phillips. *The Art & Architecture of the Aztec and Maya*. London: Annes, 2007. Print. 59.

6. Ibid.

Chapter 8. Fierce Warriors

1. Richard F. Townsend. *The Aztecs, Third ed*. London: Thames & Hudson, 2009. Print. 212.

2. John Pohl. *Aztec Warrior: AD 1325–1521*. Oxford, UK: Osprey, 2001. Print. 19.

3. Manuel Aguilar-Moreno. *Handbook to Life in the Aztec World*. New York: Oxford UP, 2007. Print. 103.

4. Richard F. Townsend. *The Aztecs, Third ed*. London: Thames & Hudson, 2009. Print. 217.

Chapter 9. Lasting Influence

1. "Templo Mayor and Its Symbolism." *Guggenheim*. Solomon R. Guggenheim Foundation, 2014. Web. 5 Sept. 2014.

2. David Carrasco. *The Aztecs*. New York: Oxford UP, 2012. Print. 112.

3. Richard F. Townsend. *The Aztecs, Third ed*. London: Thames & Hudson, 2009. Print. 241.

INDEX

Acamapichtli, 21
agriculture, 21, 49, 52, 73, 77
Ahuitzotl, 24
alphabet, 18
aqueduct, 71, 78–79
architecture, 49, 57–58
art, 17–18, 40, 54–55,
    58–59, 64, 92, 93, 94–95
astronomy, 14, 19, 49, 65
Atzcapotzalco, 21–23
Axayacatl, 24
Aztlán, 19

Badianus Manuscript, 76

cacao beans, 33, 35
calendar, 15, 49, 65, 67,
    68–70
calendar stone, 69
calpulli, 30, 41, 44, 48, 79, 88
causeways, 26, 74–75
Cempoala, 7
children, 30, 41, 44–45,
    46–49, 67
chinampa, 21, 77, 97
chocolate, 35, 37, 57, 97
cihuacoatl, 30

city-state, 14, 23, 24, 29,
    30, 34
clothing, 33, 40, 41, 58
Codex Mendoza, 33, 42–43,
    46, 49, 86
commoners, 24, 40, 41, 45,
    51, 56–57, 84, 85–86
Cortés, Hernán, 8–12, 14,
    25–27, 35
costumes, 10, 33, 86
court, 14, 24, 31, 34, 49
Covarrubias, Miguel, 95
crafts, 46
Culhua, 20, 21
currency, 35, 92

dance, 26, 48,
de Alvarado, Pedro, 25
disease, 27, 76

economy, 37
education, 30, 47, 48, 76
El Tajins, 14

family, 39, 40, 45–47
Florentine Codex, 56
Flower War, 89
food, 52, 56–57, 95, 97

gods, 19, 54, 61–67, 70, 71,
    80, 93, 95
government, 29, 30–31, 32,
    34, 37, 49
Great Temple. *See*
    Templo Mayor

homes, 52, 57–58, 77, 79
huey tlatoani, 24, 29,
    30–32, 37
Huitzilopochtli, 19, 62, 80

jewelry, 14, 40, 52

language, 14, 15, 19, 48, 49,
    92, 95
law, 24, 30, 34–35, 39, 49, 57

maize, 10, 18, 33, 45, 52, 56,
    64, 65, 88, 95
marketplace, 21, 36, 37,
    53, 97
marriage, 29, 41, 45
mathematics, 14, 19, 73
Maya, 14, 19, 37
medicine, 15, 75–77
men, 40, 45, 86
Mesoamerica, 14, 17–19
Mexica, 19

Mexico, Valley of, 12, 19–23
military, 11, 14, 21–22, 27, 30, 40, 48, 66, 83–89
Mixtecs, 14
Montezuma I, 23, 80
Montezuma II, 7, 8, 10–12, 14, 24–26, 40, 57, 58

Nahua, 95
Nahuatl, 15, 49, 95
nobles, 11, 21, 24, 29, 31, 36, 40–41, 44, 45, 57–58, 84, 85

Oaxaca, Valley of, 18
octli, 56, 57
ollama, 44
Olmecs, 14, 18–19
omen, 8

Paz, Octavio, 95
pictographs, 14, 34, 43, 68
poetry, 48, 95
priests, 19, 24, 40, 51, 62, 63–65, 67, 68
punishment, 34, 35, 39,44, 46–47, 56

Quetzalcoatl, 62, 64, 65

religion, 14, 18, 62–67
Rivera, Diego, 94–95

sacrifice, 24, 44, 61, 65–67, 71, 83, 95
scribes, 49
serfs, 44
slaves, 37, 44–45
spies, 37, 42
supreme council, 31, 85

taxes, 30, 34, 41
technology, 73–79
temples, 11, 12, 53, 58, 67, 70–71, 80, 92
Templo Mayor, 24, 26, 28, 58, 80, 92, 93
Tenoch, 21
Tenochtitlán, 7, 10, 11, 12, 14, 19–21, 23, 24, 25, 27, 29, 30–32, 33, 34, 35, 36, 42, 58, 66, 74, 77–78, 79, 80, 85, 88, 91, 92, 93, 95

Teotihuacáns, 14, 19, 57
Texcoco, Lake, 14, 19, 20, 23
Tezcatlipoca, 62, 67
Tezozomoc, 21, 22
Tlatelolco, 36, 91
tlatoani, 30–32, 34, 41, 85, 86, 88
Tlaxcalans, 2, 25–26
Toltecs, 14, 18, 19
trade, 21, 29, 35–37, 52
tradesmen, 52–53
transportation, 74–75
tribute, 21, 23, 29, 32–34, 40, 41, 42, 45, 49, 83, 84, 89, 92

Velázquez, Diego, 8

warfare, 83–89
warrior societies, 86
weapons, 10–11, 84, 87–88
women, 20, 40, 45, 67

Zapotecs, 14, 18

ABOUT THE AUTHOR

Karen Latchana Kenney is a Minneapolis author and editor who has written more than 90 books. She loves learning about different cultures and civilizations, especially those that flourished long ago. Some of her favorite foods—chocolate and guacamole—were gifts to the world from the ancient Aztecs. When not researching and writing her latest book, Kenney loves watching sci-fi movies, trying new recipes, and hanging out with her son and husband.